Worship
The Father is seeking

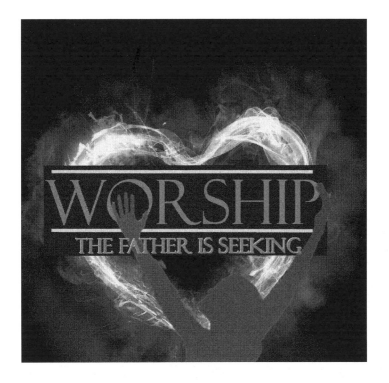

Alicia White

Chosen **S**tones
Ministries

Worship the Father is Seeking

Copyright © 2018 by Alicia White
Published by Chosen Stones Ministries
Email: info@ChosenStones.org
Web: www.chosenstones.org

All illustrations and photos are copyrighted under Chosen Stones Ministries. Without written consent, no illustrations or photos may be reproduced or copied for any reason.

Unless noted, all scripture is from the New King James Version of the Holy Bible.

No part of this book, in any form (electronic, mechanical, photocopying or recording) may be reproduced unless written consent is given in advance by the author.

Index

Dedication   4

About the Author   5

Forward   6

Introduction   7

Chapter 1: Worship War   9

Chapter 2: Worship the Father is Seeking   19

Chapter 3: Give them Purpose   27

Chapter 4: Redefining Worship   35

Chapter 5: Tabernacle Model   39

Chapter 6: Oil of Our Garments   49

Chapter 7: Moving in the Glory   53

Dedication

To my Father I dedicate this book. Since I lost my earthly Father at four, I have always found the love I was searching for in You. You did give me a wonderful earthly stepfather, I am eternally grateful for that. But ever since I could remember, Daddy, you have pursued me, even when I wasn't pursuing you. You placed in my heart a longing to please You. I have messed up in so many ways along the path, but Your grace and mercy find me. My greatest heart's desire is to lead a generation to fall as madly in love with you as I am. I know that can only happen through worship, the kind of worship you are seeking after, Father. Take my offering; use it to shift a generation's heart to worship you in spirit and in truth – to worship in the way you are seeking after.

You have my heart forever.

About the Author

Alicia White has been serving kids and families for over 12 years. She began as a children's minister of a local church plant, and slowly began to shift in her ministry focus to family. Chosen Stones Ministries was birthed in 2008 with a vision to see Malachi 4:5-6 come to pass. Alicia, in the spirit of Elijah, has a passion to see the hearts of family members return back to each other and to God. She is making a clarion call back to the ancient ways, the good path that God established for families through the 1 Peter 2:5 Priesthood. Her approach is to reestablish the family altar, through a New Testament perspective, built upon the foundation of the infilling and power of the Holy Spirit, and the truth and work of the Cross. She currently is fulfilling her ministry mandate by holding training conferences for parents and church leaders, hosting family revival services, and has been a workshop leader at conferences such as FOCUS (Church of God children ministry conference), Church of God General Assembly, and Kids in Ministry international. She has written many resources for both the church and parents, including children and family curriculum, devotionals, and her recent release of two books, *Presence-Driven Family Ministry for Your Church* and *Presence-Driven Family Worship for Your Home*. She has also written a small group curriculum for parents called *The Malachi Movement*.

Forward

As a Dove Award Nominated Songwriter and Producer I am always listening for the next thing, the next sound and the next person that will possess what God is saying in the earth. Alicia is one of the next to hit the platform to release the heart of God concerning worship. Alicia's latest book on worship is a very good read. You will sense the heart of the Father as she communicates His plan and desire for his people. Worship has so many facets and misconceptions. In today's culture our children and adults need to hear the simplicity of the gospel as it concerns worship. You will enjoy this easy read of a book and also enjoy the revelation of worshipping our Father.

Derick Thomas
Psalmist, Pastor, Worship Leader and Mentor

www.Presencedriven.tv

Introduction

Many years ago I was asked to play a part in a play for my church. Although I had never acted before, I took on the challenge to play Mary Magdalene. After the play was over the Spirit of the Lord spoke to me and said, "Alicia, will you be a worship leader for me?" My initial reaction was one I can imagine would have been from Sarah, Abraham's wife. I could not carry a tune if my life depended upon it and I had never put my hands to play an instrument. Me, a worship leader? But what the Spirit began to unfold in my heart and life years afterward was that perhaps the way we define worship is not how God defines worship at all.

After Mary, in Mark 14:3, poured her alabaster jar of perfume over Jesus, the disciples began to criticize her. But Jesus said these profound words: *"Assuredly, I say to you, wherever this gospel is preached in the whole world, what this woman has done will also be told as a memorial to her"* (Mark 14:9). Without ever singing a song or playing an instrument, Mary's worship so moved the heart of Jesus that it would be spoken in the same breath as Jesus' death, burial, and resurrection. Think about that. Of all the great men and women of the Bible – of all the signs and wonders done through their hands, and *this* women of no stature, no title or great accomplishment to speak of – has the honor of being the *only* testimony that Jesus assures worthy enough to share space with the teaching of His gospel? Wow! Worship has significant weight to the Father!

"But the hour is coming, and now is, when the true worshipers will worship the Father in spirit and truth; for the Father is seeking such to worship Him" (John 4:23). Jesus

used Mary's worship as an example for us all on how to worship in the way the Father is seeking after. The worship the Father is seeking after is not found in a song, a dance, a great beat, or a great sound – it is found in a heart that responds to the love of the Father. The way we express that is simply the act or manifestation of that worship. Worship is a matter of the heart, not of the flesh.

This leads me to very weighty questions we should all be asking ourselves as we lead children in our worship services, "Are we leading them into worship the Father is seeking after?" "Are we leading them to move the heart of Jesus?" "Are we leading them to worship with their heart, not of their flesh?"

How we lead a generation to worship, will define for them what worship is.

Join me on this journey to rediscover Biblical worship and to lead a generation into worship the Father is seeking.

Chapter 1

Worship War

"The four living creatures, each having six wings, were full of eyes around and within. And they do not rest day or night, saying: "Holy, holy, holy, Lord God Almighty, Who was and is and is to come!" Whenever the living creatures give glory and honor and thanks to Him who sits on the throne, who lives forever and ever, the twenty-four elders fall down before Him who sits on the throne and worship Him who lives forever and ever, and cast their crowns before the throne, saying: "You are worthy, O Lord, To receive glory and honor and power; For You created all things, And by Your will they exist and were created" (Revelation 4:8-11).

John, in Revelation, begins to unfold a beautiful picture of worship in heaven. This angelic/creature worship is a response to being in the presence of the Creator and His glory. If you notice, their worship does not stop; their encounter with their Creator and His power drives them into a lifestyle of worship day and night.

The end of the book reveals the beginning to us – the beginning of worship. The origin of worship did not start on earth; it started in heaven. Before you and I were ever created, angelic creatures and angels were compelled to respond to the one who created them. Nehemiah says it like this, *"You alone are the LORD; You have made heaven, The heaven of heavens, with all their host, The earth and everything on it, The seas and all that is in them, And You preserve them all. The host of heaven worships You."* (Nehemiah 9:6).

The host of heaven responded in worship to their Creator, giving Him all glory, honor, and power. But there was one who lusted after the glory of the creator, and just as worship began in heaven, so did sin. It is thought that Lucifer was the head angel of worship in heaven, based upon theologian studies in Ezekiel 28:11-16, where he was adorned with musical instruments and referred to as the anointed cherub. As the probable head worshipper, Satan saw the power of worship and began to have thoughts of rebellion in His heart towards God. In Isaiah 14:13-14, Isaiah describes what was in Satan's heart, *"For you have said in your heart: 'I will ascend into heaven, I will exalt my throne above the stars of God; I will also sit on the mount of the congregation on the farthest sides of the north;* [14] *I will ascend above the heights of the clouds, I will be like the Most High."*

> ***Satan decided he wanted to exalt himself into the place of God in order to receive God's power and glory in heaven; to be like God. This was the very first worship war that every existed.***

In fact, Revelation speaks of this worship war, *"And war broke out in heaven: Michael and his angels fought with the dragon; and the dragon and his angels fought, but they did not prevail, nor was a place found for them in heaven any longer. So the great dragon was cast out, that serpent of old, called the Devil and Satan, who deceives the whole world; he was cast to the earth, and his angels were cast out with him"* (Revelation 12:7-9). Now, some Revelation Biblical studies place this event during the tribulation time, separate from when Satan was first kicked out of heaven. The activities in Revelation often mirror that of Genesis, redeeming what was lost, so that makes sense. However, whether it was the same event or separate, it was Satan who engaged in the first worship war in heaven even before you and I existed.

This act of rebellion and sin caused Satan to get kicked out of heaven along with one-third of the angels (Revelation 12:4). Satan's rebellion against God introduced perverted and twisted worship away from its original intent. Satan now had all glory, power, and honor given to him by his fallen angels; creating the kingdom of darkness. And they were on earth, awaiting the opportunity to increase their kingdom and influence in the only way they knew how – worship.

The time had come. God desired to create again. But this creation would far exceed what was on the earth or above the earth.

> **It was the first creation that would be after His heart not His power. God desired to be much more than a Creator; He desired to be a Father.**

"So God created man in His own image; in the image of God He created him; male and female He created them" (Genesis 1:27). Humanity was birthed. God's love was poured out and manifested through a son and daughter who looked like and acted like Him. He gave them authority over the things of the earth and commanded them to multiply (Genesis 1:28).

God was in reset mode. He would create heaven on earth through His children who had His heart.

> ***Worship took a shift from angelic worship to Sonship worship.***

Now I want to explain what I mean by that so that it does not get misunderstood. God's glory and power is worth worshipping Him for, but should never be the basis for our worship. He is our Creator and holds all power, and all glory is for Him alone, yes. We should celebrate and praise Him for what He has done and continues to do in our lives. But He does these things, because He is our Father and loves us. God created humanity through a perspective of a Father.

In Hebrews, it speaks of this when comparing the angels to Jesus. Hebrews 1:4 says, *"Having become so much better than the angels, as He has by inheritance obtained a more excellent name than they."* And then it goes on to list some of the ways that Jesus was considered higher (better) than the angels. One of the ways is in Hebrews 1:5, *"For to which of the angels did He ever say: 'You are My Son, Today I have begotten You?' And again: 'I will be to Him a Father, and He shall be to Me a Son?'"* Notice the context of which he compares Jesus to the angels. It was the honor to know God as a Father and be His child that separated the angels from Jesus. And although we are not Jesus, we too, are God's sons and daughters through Christ: *"And because you are sons, God has sent forth the Spirit of His Son into your hearts, crying out, 'Abba, Father!' Therefore you are no longer a slave but a son, and if a son, then an heir of God through Christ"* (Galatians 4:6-7). This was to be a humanities position of worship throughout eternity. In fact it was Jesus' position of worship. Jesus spoke of God as

Father far more than He ever did as creator. In John alone, He spoke of Him 156 times as Father.

> **God set in motion, the day He created Adam and Eve, worship that would no longer be defined as a response to a Creator, but a response to the love of the Father.**

Worship established as fully relational and driven by love. Like any Father, God desired His children's love and presence. An earthly Father does not desire his children to love him because he can give them money, or food, or things. That is conditional love. He desires his children to love him because they are part of Him, and they want to be with Him and please Him. Love longs for a response of love. God, being love, is no different. As He walked and communed with Adam and Eve, worship became a lifestyle – a simple heart's response to the relationship they had with their Father. Being in the presence of their Daddy, the One who is Love; responding to His perfected, indescribable, immeasurable love had to have been easy, natural, very real, and authentic.

But Lucifer – Satan – waited for such an opportunity. Satan, understanding angelic worship, presented humanity with an opportunity – an opportunity to respond out of the glory and power of their Creator, instead of the love of the Father. Satan comes to Eve and tempts her to shift her way of thinking about God. In fact, he uses the same terminology as to what is used to describe what he was thinking when he sinned in heaven – "to be like God". When Eve's perspective shifted from relational (love) to power, she was easy prey for Satan. When Satan assured her that she would be more like God (Genesis 3:5), he was speaking of God's power. His glory. The sin in his own heart to be exalted upon God's throne, was now being transferred to humanity. Adam and Eve were already made in God's image (had His heart) – now it was a pursuit of power. Genesis 3:6 speaks of the wisdom she was after. Wisdom for what? Wisdom is power, and she desired it all.

> **When Adam and Eve disobeyed God and ate of the tree, they chose power over love – power to become their own God.**

Essentially, it was the lust of the flesh that they gave in to. Satan obtained power over humanity through one act of perverted and twisted worship. Our hearts were turned over to the Kingdom of Darkness and love Himself was separated from us. Perverted worship was introduced to humanity, and so the worship war for our heart and soul began.

Separated from walking with His children in the garden, God was grieved, not because He did not have their worship, but because He did not have their heart.

> **Whatever or whomever you worship has your heart. That is, they hold the power over your life. Out of our heart is where life is determined and lived.**

The battle for humanity's heart has been violent and relentless. God's people in scripture turned towards idols, and with every law of worship, their hearts got more separated; only worshipping out of tradition and religion. Their hearts were not in it. The Old Testament children had no understanding of God the Father for the most part. Only a few ever encountered God's presence. Their worship was driven by God's power as their Creator, not out of love. In fact, most of time, they performed acts of worship out of fear of what God would do if they did not.

Even those who claimed to "love" God, could not even recognize Him when He came. Jesus was not worshipped by the masses, because He held no earthly power or authority. The children of God no longer knew how to respond to the love of the Father even when it was standing right in front of them. Humanity's worship was defined by a perverted perspective Satan has planted in their hearts thousands of years past in the garden.

Only the few who communed with Jesus, who walked with Him and talked with Him – surrendered their heart to Him in worship. This is why Jesus came. Jesus' purpose for coming to earth was far beyond coming to die for our sins, that was only the way in which His purpose was lived out. Jesus' purpose was to bring us back to the Father. Ephesians 2:13 say, *"But now in Christ Jesus you who once were far off have been brought near by the blood of Christ."* He was the manifestation of God's love on earth to all of humanity.

> ***Jesus brought us back to the heart of worship –***
> ***a life spent and heart's response***
> ***to the love of the Father.***

So where are we in the present day worship war? "Worship wars" have become a Christianized slogan for the lust of self-gods and power seated deep within the flesh of humanity today. We have made worship about everything but the love of the Father. The war manifests often in our adult sanctuaries, and the private conversations of those who attend. The elders want to hear the songs they grew up with, and the young want the new sound with words that connect to their generation. Leaders and Pastors who seek to please have split their services (essentially their church) into two; traditional and modern. And many who have stayed the course with one service, try their best to please everyone by blending two styles of music together. Leaders walk a fine line between pleasing man and God, and in many of these cases, man wins out. We have lost the heart of worship.

This place of division in the church really isn't about music or what generation knows how to worship the best. The true war is going on within the hearts of God's children who have taken a bite out of what Satan was selling in the garden. We are in a worship crisis. A worship war yes, but not perhaps in the way we have previously thought about it. The mindsets and behaviors concerning the fundamental doctrine of worship have already been formed before we enter adulthood and simulate into adult worship. What concerns me about what I see in the adult services, is that I don't think it started there. Satan is after the heart of a generation. He gets their worship. He gets their heart. He is warring for the hearts of our children, and it's time to get in the battle!

The worship war is all about the heart. Today there is a tug-of-war for a generation's heart at every turn. Technology and rapid advancement in today's society and church culture are pressing down upon our children, distracting them and their families from the Father's heart. It has become too easy in the western world to stroke the flesh. Satan has a pretty easy job today when it comes to warring for our worship. And the generation we see arising in our kid's church are so used to being entertained in the flesh – that to do anything else is a war in itself. But we must.

> *We must fight against the grain of the world and church culture and programs. Fight against tradition and religion to see a generation who will choose love of the Father over the flesh. It will take intentional effort to fight this spiritual battle – are you ready and willing?*

Chapter 2

Worship the Father is Seeking

If we are going to engage in the worship war battle and bring a generation back to the heart of worship the Father is seeking after, it has to start with a Biblical foundation. I want us to really begin to build a foundation for Biblical, New Testament, worship – worship defined from the Fathers perspective.

"Jesus said to her, "Woman, believe Me, the hour is coming when you will neither on this mountain, nor in Jerusalem, worship the Father. You worship what you do not know; we know what we worship, for salvation is of the Jews. But the hour is coming, and now is, when the true worshipers will worship the Father in spirit and truth; for the Father is seeking such to worship Him. God is Spirit, and those who worship Him must worship in spirit and truth" (John 4:21-24).

As I previously mentioned in the last chapter, Jesus came to do so much more than to merely forgive us of our sins. He came to bring us back to the Father – to restore our heart of worship. Notice how God is referred to as "Father" in the context of worship in this scripture. Jesus' conversation with the woman at the well reveals the Father's heart for His children. He is seeking after a generation who knows *in Whom* they worship. A generation who worships out of relationship – not tradition or religion.

> ***However you lead a generation into worship, will be how you define worship to them.***

If I want to do anything as a leader, I want to lead a generation into worship whom the Father is seeking after.

God is spirit and that requires us to worship Him in Spirit. What does that mean? I want to take us back to a scripture, *"And because you are sons, God has sent forth the Spirit of His Son into your hearts, crying out, 'Abba, Father!' Therefore you are no longer a slave but a son, and if a son, then an heir of God through Christ" (Galatians 4:6-7).* It is through the Spirit of Christ in us that we worship the Father. The Holy Spirit bears witness in us as a son or daughter and we cry out for Daddy God. It is the Sonship perspective.

We all too often expect kids to worship a God somewhere out there in the universe they have not seen or experienced. Worship must be experiential. You must introduce them to the third party of the trinity. The Holy Spirit is essential in spirit worship. He brings the reality of Jesus to the present, so that children have a person to worship. Do not be afraid to speak of the Spirit of God. I have heard people who think if you talk about the Holy Spirit during worship, you are worshipping Him instead of Jesus. That is wrong theology.

> ***The person of the Holy Spirit is Jesus on earth. Right now, in the present day, He is the most important part of the trinity for us.***

Why do I say that? Without Him you can't be saved (John 6:44), encounter Jesus (Romans 8:9, John 14:15), or draw near to the Father (Ephesians 2:13). The Spirit of God on the inside of us is our connection to Abba Father. The angels only have God physically with them, whereas, we have Abba Father living on the inside of us.

In order to lead a generation into worship the Father is seeking after, we must teach them to recognize and press through to the Spirit. This is one-half of the worship war battle – the battle of our flesh. We must continually point them to Daddy, Abba Father – inside of them – that they may commune and dwell with Him.

All too often, as we lead children into worship, it is defined by what feels good, what connects to children's souls, and what we have always done traditionally. This feeds right into the mindsets manifested in the adult worship wars going on today.

> ***In any given kids worship service we may have lyrics on a screen, music videos, and hand motions. This is what I call "Outer Court" worship.***

The Outer Court of the Tabernacle was all about the flesh; the flesh of Jesus and the flesh of humanity. We will discuss that much more in detail later. It was a necessary place of worship, but not a place to stay. The Father is seeking after those who will worship Him in Spirit, not in the flesh. Music videos, fun beats, and high active dance motions – all connect children in the flesh. Often this type of worship opens up children's hearts. That is a good place to start. But the Father is seeking after those who will go further.

There are many different reasons why we lead children into

Outer Court worship and stay there. I believe one of the main reasons is because we are just trying to do anything to get the kids engaged and moving. There is nothing worse than seeing little eyes stare you down as you try to sing and lead them into a worship moment. I believe we also are at a loss on how to lead kids into authentic worship. Later in this book I will be given you a step-by-step blueprint on how to do just that. I also believe we are leading kids in this type of worship because that is all we have ever known. It is based upon tradition. Lastly, I believe in many cases, it is because, we ourselves, do not have a Father-focused worship perspective.

Whatever the reason may be *why* we lead children in Outer Court worship only, and stay there – it has made determinate effects on the entire body. Think about this. Have you ever went and observed one of your children who have graduated to junior high/youth? How did they participate in worship? With the exception of a few, most talk with their friends or stand there in silence with their hands crossed or to their side. At most, they may sing, but with little or no expression of true worship. Why would we expect anything less? If they have grown up in church, what they know about worship and how to respond to it has come through you and me as children's leaders or parents. How have we defined worship for them or taught them to worship? With no fun hand or feet motions, catchy beats with "light weight" and simple lyrics – they are simply lost. They do not know how to press in and respond out of their heart to the Father's love. Once a child hits their teen years, it is incredibly hard to engage them beyond peer pressure and self-awareness.

> ***Without the sovereign grace of God, teenagers who have not already made worship a lifestyle and a common activity, will most likely continue to see worship from the Outer Court. As they grow into adults, they will choose either not to engage, or to stick their fist in the battle of worship -- making it all about their flesh not about the Spirit.***

We must seek after getting out of our boxes and leading a generation into worship the Father is seeking after. It is time to take them beyond the Outer Court and encounter the presence of the Father. He longs to be with them. We have hindered that in so many ways.

As we evaluate the idea of worship in the Spirit we must ask ourselves, are they connecting with the Holy Spirit on the inside of them and are they driven by the Father's love? Do your children encounter the Holy Spirit when they worship? Do they know Who they worship because they have been with Him?

Jesus refers to this speaking to the women at the well, *"You worship what you do not know..."* (John 4:22). More times than not, when we refer to God in our kids' services, we refer to Him as our Creator, Savior, and King... maybe... and for sure the God of power. However, how often do we refer to Him as Father, Daddy, and Abba?

> **Could it be we have inadvertently given them a bite of the fruit that seeks after the lust of the flesh? Have we shifted the perspective of which a generation sees God? Is the worship we are defining for them... relational... or flesh driven? Are we inviting them to commune with the Father; to walk with Him and talk with Him as Adam and Eve did?**

The second half of the worship war battle is leading a generation to worship in truth. What does Jesus mean by worshiping in truth? It all comes back to God's desire to "reset" in the garden. He desired a creation that would be after His own heart – a people who would be real and genuine in their worship to Him. Those who would worship out of their hearts, a response to the love and presence of the Father. A people who would make worship a lifestyle, not just a place they go. Jesus referred to this when speaking to the women at the well, *"Woman, believe Me, the hour is coming when you will neither on this mountain, nor in Jerusalem, worship the Father"* (John 4:21).

Worship is a matter of the heart. As New Testament believers, we are both the temple (1 Corinthians 6:19) and the Priest (1 Peter 2:5). We are the resting place of the Father and we have access to Him at any time. Worship has become a "church" thing not a "life" thing. We have made it about the songs we sing, when more often than not we are not singing them from our heart. Children half the time do not even understand what they are singing – they are just regurgitating what they see on a screen.

> **There is no doubt we live in a fatherless generation. According to the U.S. Census Bureau, 1 out of 4 children are being raised without a father in their lives.**

And if you think those statistics don't reflect the church, you are sadly mistaken. And in my opinion, we are suffering from a parentless generation. Those mothers who are left to raise their children alone, have to spend the majority of their time providing for their family. And in the majority of the married households, both parents work. The family altar is almost non-existent in the church and at home. Children today need a Father who will be ever-present in their lives. One they can be real with and be confident in the love He has for them. God longs for us to introduce a generation to their Father. They need it even more so today than in any other generation. Worship, in truth, is simply coming to the Father in authenticity and relationship. It is time we introduce them to their Daddy. God is waiting for His children, *"I will be a Father to you, And you shall be My sons and daughters, Says the LORD Almighty."* (2 Corinthians 6:18).

Chapter 3

Give them Purpose

Over the many years of ministering to kids and families in presence-driven worship, I have found several key principles that have help me lead a generation into worship the Father is seeking after. In the several chapters, I am going to break down for you this step-by-step process you can use to make a shift in your kids worship services. This chapter we are going to explore giving a generation a purpose for their worship.

"To what purpose is the multitude of your sacrifices to Me?" Says the LORD. "I have had enough of burnt offerings of rams and the fat of fed cattle. I do not delight in the blood of bulls, Or of lambs or goats" (Isaiah 1:11).

I don't think the majority of the children, or even adults, in our churches understand why we do what we do in worship.

> **It is almost nearly impossible to get someone to authentically engage in worship when they have no purpose for it. Yet, this is what we are trying to do week after week throughout the body.**

We force kids (even adults) to stand up, sing the song we put on the screen, and move their hands and feet because that is just what we do in worship. Do we even know, as leaders, *why* we do what we do? We have made worship such a tradition, that we have lost our purpose for it.

In Isaiah, God was speaking to His children that offered up sacrifices and called it worship. They often mixed their worship to God with idols, and they are participating in acts of worship, without the *heart* of worship. With all my heart, I believe that this is where so many of our churches are today.

> **We are leading a generation who has no understanding of worship, no Biblical foundation or teaching, and they simply are going through the motions to please others and do what is asked of them.**

This reminds me of a story in scripture. Not just a story, or an example, but a warning for us as leaders. In Leviticus 10:1-2 *"Nadab and Abihu, the sons of Aaron, each took his censer and put fire in it, put incense on it, and offered profane fire before the LORD, which He had not commanded them. So fire went out from the LORD and devoured them, and they died before the LORD."* Aaron's sons had watched and participated in the acts of worship with their Father for years, but lacked the understanding or relationship with their heavenly Father to engage in authentic worship. The scripture tells us that God had not commanded them to offer up burnt incense, yet they did it anyways. They did not seek the voice of God or have purpose in their act of worship – they performed it out of tradition and religion. Their worship was not relational or out of the heart, this is what I fear for the generation we are raising. My fear is that we are inadvertently leading a generation into profane fire.

Step one in ever getting a generation to worship in the way the Father is seeking, is to give them a purpose for their worship. Help them discover the reason why we do what we do in worship.

We have inadvertently defined the purpose of worship to a generation to be something that is demanded of us as if to stroke our God's ego. We have painted this picture of this God in heaven who needs to have people tell Him how good he is. God never needs His ego stroked; He is who He is whether we say it to Him or not. He does not need us to worship Him, He desires us to do so. *"Have the people of Israel build me a holy sanctuary so I can live among them"* (Exodus 25:8). The sanctuary is the place of worship and we have become that sanctuary. God created worship to be with His children; a roadway to His presence. In fact, it is the only way to God's presence.

> ***The purpose of our worship should always be to bring the children into an encounter with the Father.***

To give them opportunity to feel, touch, and hear the manifestation of the Holy Spirit; Jesus made real in them. I would like to encourage you, right before you lead your children into worship to remind them of this purpose. I often use this as an example: *"If you are going to visit a friend would you have to take steps to get there? Possibly call them, drive to their home, or ring their doorbell? We are about to take the steps to be with Jesus and the Father. He is waiting on you and can't wait to talk to you and be with you. The more you enter in and give Him all your attention and heart, is the more you can encounter Him."* It's amazing the response you get when kids believe they can encounter the Father.

I want to stop right here and explain the difference between praise and worship. Both have purpose, but they take on very different roles. If we are not careful we will lead a generation into praise never bringing them to worship.

Praise is an Outer Court response of the love of the Father. It is a manifestation of Psalm 100:4, *"Enter into His gates with thanksgiving, And into His courts with praise."* It is a much-needed response. Praise does two things essentially. It opens the door to our soul (mind, will, and emotions), which prepares us to be in line with God's truth. Secondly, it opens the door to heaven preparing us for an encounter. Praise is always the first response in worship, as it realigns us with the Father through the Spirit of Christ. Praise was created to be a bridge to worship.

> **Praise realigns us to the Father, but worship brings the reality of the Father to our present. Praise reaches up to heaven.**
> **Worship brings heaven to earth.**

Worship in spirit and in truth is an exchange of this earth for heaven. A perfect place to see this illustrated is in the very first scripture that speaks of worship; Genesis 22, the story of Abraham bringing his son to Moriah to be offered as a sacrifice. Abraham says to the two young men with him, *"Stay here with the donkey; the lad and I will go yonder and worship, and we will come back to you* (Genesis 22:5)." Abraham exchanged earth for heaven that day. Surrender brought him to a place of sacrifice, and sacrifice brought him to a place of exchange. This is the difference between praise and worship. Worship will always cost you something. Abraham was tested by God that day to see if He was willing to move from praise to worship. Isaac was not only flesh of his flesh, but he also had the love of his daddy's heart. When we surrender all of our flesh, all of our heart, all we love, we receive the blessing of the Lamb.

> ***Jesus is waiting for you, me, and this generation, to come up to the mountain and worship so He can give more of Himself to us.***

God said to Abraham, *"By Myself I have sworn, says the LORD, because you have done this thing, and have not withheld your son, your only son-- blessing I will bless you, and multiplying I will multiply your descendants as the stars of the heaven and as the sand which is on the seashore; and your descendants shall possess the gate of their enemies (Genesis 22:16-17)."* The purpose of worship, yes, is more of Jesus, but in that exchange, we get the blessings of heaven. There is never been a greater time in history where a generation needs to possess the gates of their enemies. We can't afford to raise a generation who only sees what Jesus has done from afar off. When we "camp out" at praise we are unintentionally teaching a generation to align themselves with the Father and the truth of the gospel, but never teaching them to surrender. Praise is about what the Father gave through Jesus, worship is about what we give. It is possible to believe in Jesus without picking up your cross and following: *"Then you will begin to say, 'We ate and drank in Your presence, and You taught in our streets. But He will say, 'I tell you I do not know you, where you are from. Depart from Me, all you workers of iniquity' (Luke 13:26-27)."* Without the exchange of worship, we will raise a generation to know truth and even speak it with their mouth, but their heart will be far from it. Leap service at best. There will be a false since of worship that does not require a sacrifice, and this in return will cause a lack of intimacy, relationship, and surrender towards Jesus and the Father.

Part of teaching a generation about the purpose of their worship, is to invest time to teach on worship. Worship is a fundamental doctrine of the church, and our relationship with Jesus and the Father, yet how often do we teach on this subject? Several years ago I put together a curriculum called *Radical Worship*. This 13-week curriculum takes children through the origins of worship, to why we must worship, how worship changes us from the inside out, and lastly goes through the Tabernacle of Moses and lays out a blueprint of worship ordained by God.

> ***The more we can teach children about this fundamental doctrine and principle of worship we are to practice in our walk as Christians, the more we will see the fruit of a generation who is engaged in genuine worship.***

Devote a quarter of the year to teaching your children about Biblical worship.

Let's go a bit further even. I also would like to encourage you, right before you lead your children into worship each Sunday, to explain to them what you are about to do and why. When I am leading kids, I am always teaching them about why we are doing a particular act of worship. We have many actions, or what I call acts of worship in the body. Tackle one each week and teach them about it. Then, invite them to engage in that particular worship. I have many examples of this in my resource called *Acts of Worship*. It is a curriculum intended to be used right before your worship experience with the kids. It gives you a mini-object lesson on a particular type of worship, and an activity to engage in that worship in a creative way. As you teach children about why we do what we do in worship, it gives them a target; a purpose for their worship. With an understanding and a heart of worship, they then can engage fully in Biblical and authentic worship the Father is seeking. The mini-lessons I use in my *Acts of Worship* curriculum all have objects lessons that connect the dots between the natural and supernatural. Just like you would use objects or activities to connect children during the lesson of your day, use them in worship. Communion is one of the biggest object lessons in scripture, yet it is worship. Communion is a worship expression that draws us into the presence of God and brings the reality of the cross into our present. We can use this type of tool for all kinds of worship.

> ***Connecting the dots between the natural and spiritual realm is important to make worship personal and relational.***

I want to share with you some examples of what a mini-worship lesson and activation could look like. These are excerpts from my *Acts of Worship* resource and are not being shared in their entirety:

Making Jesus Bigger
"...will magnify Him with thanksgiving." Psalms 69:30

Object: Magnifying Glass

Main Idea: When you offer thanksgiving unto Jesus, you are magnifying Him, or making Him bigger in your life and to others around you.

Act of Worship: Give each child a deflated balloon that represents Jesus. As they shout out what they are thankful for, they get to blow in the balloon, making Jesus bigger. Let them hit the balloon up in the air during worship.

Making a Funnel
"In the last days, I will pour out my Spirit upon all people."
Acts 2:17

Object: Large funnel

Main Idea: A funnel is an object used to pour something very large into something very small. God is a big, big, God and He desires to pour into you. When you raise your hands to Him you are inviting Him to do so.

Act of Worship: Encourage the kids to raise their hands and create a funnel for Jesus to pour into them.

Worship that Goes Up
"Your prayers and gifts to the poor have been received by God as an offering." Acts 10:3

Object: Pictures of memorials

Main Idea: Retell the story of Cornelius in Acts 10:4. A memorial is a reminder of something important.

Act of Worship: Place a building block in front of the room. Invite each child to come up and pray in the mic. After praying, each child gets to add their block to yours, making a memorial before the Lord of all the prayers.

Chapter 4

Redefining Worship

I want to bring you back to a story I spoke of in my introduction of the book. It is a powerful story, but much more than that. It is a living manifestation of worship the Father is seeking after. The story of Mary and her alabaster jar. After Mary, in Mark 14:3, poured her alabaster jar of perfume over Jesus, the disciples began to criticize her. But Jesus said these profound words: *"Assuredly, I say to you, wherever this gospel is preached in the whole world, what this woman has done will also be told as a memorial to her"* (Mark 14:9).

> **Without ever singing a song or playing an instrument, Mary's worship, driven by a heart's response to the love of the Father, so moved the heart of Jesus that it would be spoken in the same breath as Jesus' death, burial, and resurrection.**

Think about that. Of all the great men and women of the Bible, all the signs and wonders done through their hands, and this women of no stature, no title or great accomplishment to speak of, has the honor of being the only testimony that Jesus assures worthy enough to share space with the teaching of His gospel. This is worship in Spirit and in Truth. This is worship the Father is seeking after.

We have wrapped worship up in music for as long as I can remember, especially in children's church. Unknowingly, we have defined worship to a generation to be a song we sing. Yes, music is a Biblical *response* of worship, but it is just that; a response. Again, we come back to redefining worship as a heart's response to the love of the Father. Everything we do, how we serve, how we speak, how we live, the choices we make, talking with Jesus, soaking in His presence, listening for His voice, praying for people – are all responses to the love of the Father. He so loved us that He sent His son who died so we could live, and be reunited with our Daddy. Jesus, the Father manifested on earth through flesh and blood, gave it all for us. Love so great, it should compel us to give Him our all.

Worship is so much more than a song. We need to stop compartmentalizing worship, making it so much less than what it should be. Worship is to be a twenty-four-seven lifestyle. We are the New Testament Priest according to 1 Peter 2:4, *"Coming to Him as to a living stone, rejected indeed by men, but chosen by God and precious, you also, as living stones, are being built up a spiritual house, a holy priesthood, to offer up spiritual sacrifices acceptable to God through Jesus Christ."* And as I mentioned earlier – we are also the temple. We are to be walking worshippers where ever we go and whatever we do. Worship does not end at the end of the slow song. Mary's worship moved the heart of Jesus; this is the worship we should be leading our children in.

> **_Let's move beyond the two fast songs and one slow song, hand motions, and singing lyrics off of a screen. Instead, intentionally pursue leading children into many responses of the heart to the love of the Father._**

Including music and singing yes, but not always, and not only. Worship needs to be a lifestyle – not only a Sunday morning event. Most leaders would agree that obedience, prayer, serving, even listening for the voice of God, would be worship. Yet, we do none of those things within the confines of the worship portion of our services with children.

> **_God does not intend for us to teach children that they must all worship one way, like we are raising some kind of robot clones. It's time to open of the box and let the creativity of the Holy Spirit lead us into redefining worship for a generation._**

I want to share a few examples of responses of worship from my *Acts of Worship* curriculum that emphasizes activities outside of singing. These are excerpts and not the lessons in their entirety. Use music in these cases in the background to create atmosphere:

- ➤ Have kids that need prayer come up and have other kids lay hands on them and pray (use this as an opportunity to teach them to pray for the sick).

- ➤ Have them sit in their chairs while listening for the voice of God. They are to write down every single thing they think of. Invite them to read off their list.

99% of the time you will find that kids will start out thinking carnally like "I am hungry," but by the end of the list, God will start speaking to them. They learn that God is speaking; we just have to get through all the noise to hear Him.

➢ Have an open mic (kids love speaking in a mic) and invite the kids to come up and say what they are thankful for or have them say what they praise Jesus for.

➢ Have scriptures printed out for each child. Have them walk around the room and pray and even sing the scripture (a wonderful opportunity to teach them how to declare and pray the word).

➢ Pass out a large paper heart to each child, and as they sit in the presence of God, encourage them to write down what they want to say to Him. Take time to share.

All these things and more are worship. Mary and her alabaster box was an example for leading children in worship. It was her genuine heart's response to the love of the Father that moved her into the pages of eternity.

> ***The weight of our ministry to children is heavy, but let it be said about us, that we taught a generation how to move the heart of the Father through worship, that their impact may remain throughout eternity.***

Chapter 5

The Tabernacle Model

"And let them make Me a sanctuary, that I may dwell among them" (Exodus 25:8).

Time and time again, we see the struggle of a Father who desired to be with His children, but sin has separated us. Abba would not give up. In the wilderness, He decided to bring heaven to earth through the Tabernacle of Moses. He prepared the way to be with His children.

> **When God instructed Moses to build the Tabernacle, he had His children in mind.**

From the number of furniture pieces (6), which represents humanity, to each posture of worship, God gave us a pattern of worship that would lead us right into the Father's presence.

The tabernacle of Moses consisted of three major areas; the Outer Court, the Inner Court or Sanctuary, and Inner Most Court or the most Holy place. These three places are identified in the trinity of God: Father, Son, and Holy Spirit.

Each section represents a separate part of the trinity. As we are also the Tabernacle, each section represents us as well: body, soul, and spirit.

If we use what God has put in His word, it will do the work for us, and we will see the fruit of it manifested in this generation. The Tabernacle model is a pattern for us – a step-by-step process. In this chapter, I want to break down for you each room of the Tabernacle, each furniture piece, what it represents, and how you can use this blueprint in sequence to draw your children into the presence of the Father. This is only a pattern though. Most importantly, we are to allow the Spirit to lead us.

The following information about the Tabernacle rooms and furniture pieces are excerpts from my *Radical Worship curriculum* for children's ministry.

The Outer Court:

The Outer Court consisted of a cloth fence that contained the altar of burnt offerings and the bronze laver. This area was completely uncovered. It was lit by the natural light of the sun. This was a foreshadowing of God's Son (sun) that was to be the light of the world (John 8:12). The Outer Court also represented the flesh of humanity. This was a place of high activity and noise.

- ➤ The Altar of Sacrifice: The very first furniture piece we come to in the Outer Court. The animals would be brought in and taken to the altar to be sacrificed. Of course we know that Christ, as the Lamb of God, fulfilled this requirement on the cross once and for all (John 1:29). The foreshadowing of the Altar of Sacrifice does not stop with Jesus. The altar in us represents the death and sacrifice of our flesh as we live through Christ. Jesus said in Luke 9:23 that we must deny ourselves and take up our own cross (altar). This place of surrender is what brings us close to God's presence again in worship.

Altar of Sacrifice Worship: This is where you can best use all of the fun, high praise, hand motion songs we are so used to in children's church. This connects kids flesh and helps engage them. Use worship songs or responses of worship that are centered on Christ, the cross, and our surrender to Him.

Example of Worship: Communion. Usually an act of worship done at the end of service, but it is actually considered an Outer Court worship experience.

> Bronze Laver: The next step of worship through the tabernacle of Moses in the Outer Court is the Bronze Laver. The bronze laver was basically a very large bowl made out of bronze filled with water. The Priest would come over to the washbasin after sacrificing the animal and wash his hands and feet of the blood that had gotten on him during the sacrificial act of worship. We experience Christ's death at the altar of sacrifice, but we experience His life at the bronze laver. The bronze laver represents the born again experience for us. It also can represent the baptism of the Holy Spirit who works to empower us to become more like Christ and to testify of Christ to others.

Bronze Laver Worship: You can focus on the baptism of the Holy Spirit here as well as Christ resurrection power.

Example of Worship: Encourage time where the kids can linger, singing in the Spirit. Pray for those who desire the baptism during this time.

The Inner Court:

We are going to move from the outer court into the inner court. This was the first of two rooms enclosed in the tent of the Tabernacle. The only light in this room would come from the Lampstand. The Lampstand was fueled with oil, which represents the Holy Spirit of the Trinity. This room focuses on the Holy Spirit of the Trinity and is about the work of ministry in us and through our souls. This room is all about partnering with the Holy Spirit.

> ➤ The Lampstand: The first furniture piece in this room. The Lampstand represents many postures of worship. One is to uncover hidden things in our hearts. Proverbs 20:27 says, *"The spirit of a man is the lamp of the LORD, Searching all the inner depths of his heart."* This is what David was asking for in Psalms 139:23 when he asked God to search him. It's a place of sanctification and receiving the mind of Christ. The second foreshadowing of the lampstand in us is the Holy Spirit bringing us into revelation of who God is and what His word means. The light of the Holy Spirit illuminates hidden things within God's word and Kingdom to reveal to us deeper revelation of who He is and who we are to Him (Luke 8:10). Lastly, this place is a reflection of the light in us, *"You are the light of the world. A city that is set on a hill cannot be hidden. "Nor do they light a lamp and put it under a basket, but on a lampstand, and it gives light to all who are in the house." Let your light so shine before men, that they may see your good*

works and glorify your Father in heaven" (Matt 5:14-16).

Lampstand Worship: Worship here can take on many different aspects, as there is so much reflection here at this place. It is the place of God's revelation, changing of the heart, and the ministry of the Holy Spirit.

Example of Worship: Allowing opportunity for the gifts of the Spirit to come forth (prophecy, interpretation of tongues, gift of healing and miracles, etc.). Let the children minister one to another.

➤ Table of Showbread: The second place of worship in the inner court. It was simply a table that the priest would display the bread and grain offerings from the people (exodus 25:23). To begin to explore the foreshadowing revealed at this table, we must look at a story in the Bible found in Exodus 16. The Israelites were stuck in the wilderness, tired and hungry. They had already forgotten the promise of God to bring them into a land filled with milk and honey. So the Bible says that God heard their complaints and rained down bread from heaven for them to eat every day. Exodus 16:31 says it was like coriander seed and tasted like honey. The interesting thing about this seed is that it is white like milk and it tasted like honey, which sounds a lot like their promise from God to be given a land filled with milk and honey (Exodus 3:8). So, at first glance we can see how the bread on the table of showbread spiritually was a reminder of the promises of God. Today we don't have bread raining down from heaven, but what we do have to eat to remind us of the promises of God, is the Word of God.

Table of Showbread Worship: Here it is all about the Word of God. But not just about the reading of the Word, but experiencing the Word.

Example of Worship: Have a large loaf of bread in the front of the room and invite each person to come up and declare a promise of God in His word. Each person that does can have a piece of the bread, which represents eating of the word.

➢ Altar of Incense: The last piece of furniture in the Inner Court. The Altar of Incense is where the priest was required to burn incense day and night (Exodus 30:7-8). Ephesians 5:2 tells us, *"walk in love, as Christ also has loved us and given Himself for us, an offering and a sacrifice to God for a sweet-smelling aroma."* When we express God's love – that is worship – and that worship has the power to create an aroma. As incense was burned, a cloud of smoke would bellow out from it. This smoke is a foreshadowing of God's presence (Exodus 13:21). James 4:8 says that as we draw near to God, He draws near to us. This means as we worship, it produces God's presence – the Holy Spirit. As we lift up our hands, sing praises to Him, as we share God's love with others, as we obey His word – His presence comes down and lifts our worship up to God. Worship is not only expressing our love to God, it is expressing God's love to others.
Psalms 141:2 says, *"Let my prayer be set before You as incense, The lifting up of my hands as the evening sacrifice"*. The Altar of Incense is where we get to worship God through intercession.

Altar of Incense Worship: In this place of worship the Father's presence begins to take over and we use our own mouths to bring heaven to earth through intercession and acts of worship.

Example of Worship: Use incense in the room. Have each child come up and pray over it in a mic. You can either have subjects to direct them or allow them to intercede for things as the Holy Spirit burdens them.

The Most Holy Place

The last room of the Tabernacle was a place the Priest could only enter into one time of the year. It is the most holy place where God's presence, His glory, was the only thing that illuminated this room. As Christ fulfilled the law, the veil was torn and now we can enter in freely as the Priest of God. This place represents the Father, and in us, our spirits.

> ➢ Ark of the Covenant: The only furniture in this room. It was the box that was believed to be the house of the Presence of God. There were requirements to get into this room. The priest had to have blood from the altar and incense from the Inner Court. The Bible says in Hebrew 10:19-20, *"Therefore, brethren, having boldness to enter the Holiest by the blood of Jesus, by a new and living way which He consecrated for us, through the veil, that is, His flesh."* Today there is still a veil we must go through; the blood of the Lamb of God that we received at the altar of sacrifice. And guess what, we still need the incense which produces the Holy Spirit found at the altar of our worship. There are no shortcuts to get to the

Father, but when we do, the fullness of the trinity is represented. The Most Holy place is where we do nothing and God does everything. In the outer and inner court something was required of us, but once we step into this room, God does all the work and we simply receive. In 1 Kings 8:11, this is what happened to the priest as the cloud of God's glory filled the tent. God's glory, His character and nature are received in this place. It is also the place of His voice. *"There I will meet with you, and I will speak with you from above the mercy seat, from between the two cherubim which are on the Ark of the Testimony"* (Exodus 25:22).

Ark of the Covenant Worship: This is your target. This is the place where worship becomes about the love of the Father. Worship in this place will take on a holy moment that can't be replicated.

Example of Worship: Allow the kids to soak in the presence of God and listen for him to speak or minister. Give them opportunity to share.

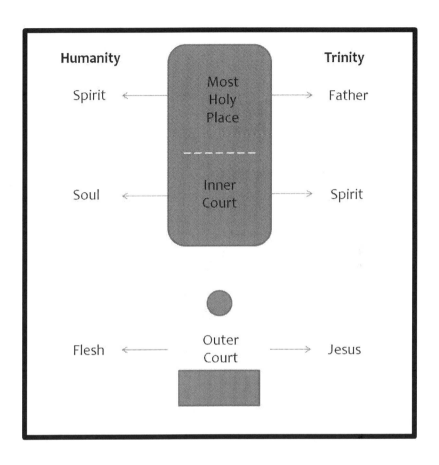

Outer Court	Inner Court	Most Holy Place
Worship focus in these rooms		
Blood of Christ	Sanctification	Father's Love
The Work of the Cross	Revelation	Voice of God
Surrender	Gifts of the Spirit	Peace
Baptisms of the Spirit	Word of God	Joy
	Intercession	Hiding Place

Chapter 6

"Behold, how good and how pleasant it is for brethren to dwell together in unity! It is like the precious oil upon the head, running down on the beard, the beard of Aaron, Running down on the edge of his garments (Psalm 133:1-2)."

There is something very profound in this scripture, that when uncovered, reveals to us one of the key principles in seeing a generation worship the Father. I need to spend some time and break down this scripture for us.

Aaron is the appointed high Priest in the Old Testament. But the Priesthood was not a "me" thing, it was a "we" thing. As it says in Exodus 40:14-15, *"And you shall bring his sons and clothe them with tunics. You shall anoint them, as you anointed their father, that they may minister to Me as priests; for their anointing shall surely be an everlasting priesthood throughout their generations."*

> **Aaron's sons were anointed as their Father was, and they ministered as their Father did.**

We already discussed the mistake Aaron made when raising his children to worship without purpose. But I want us to focus on the oil of their Father; the oil of the Priesthood.

Aaron represented God's establishment of the earthly Priesthood. What God establishes in the Old Testament is always fulfilled in the New. *"Coming to Him as to a living stone, rejected indeed by men, but chosen by God and precious, you also, as living stones, are being built up a spiritual house, a holy priesthood, to offer up spiritual sacrifices acceptable to God through Jesus Christ"* (1 Peter 2:4-5). As followers of Christ, we are the New Testament Priesthood. So now we can identify to be like Aaron in this scripture. Whether you are a parent, leader in the church, or simply and respectfully a servant of the Father, you are the Priest of God. You have oil or should have oil on your garments. This oil upon your garments, will undoubtedly, rub off onto the next generation. Whether it is your own children, or the children God has given you to minister to, as Priest you have a responsibility to the next generation of Priest. This is God's ordained order to ensure an everlasting Priesthood.

> **So the question we need to ask ourselves, is what oil is rubbing off on the next generation of worshipers? We cannot give what we have not received. Where is your walk as a worshiper? Do you worship in the way the Father is seeking? Have you simply camped out at praise and not went up to the mountain of worship?**

What I have found most about being a parent for 20 years and a children and family minister for over 13, is that where I am spiritually directly affects where my kids are spiritually. We cannot expect a generation to engage in authentic worship, in spirit and in truth, if we ourselves do not.

As leaders in the body the demand on your calling is heavy, exhausting, and eternally impactful, making the pressure overwhelming sometimes. We are so busy with programs and demands of performance, making sure we have it all together, that I wonder if we have forgotten to make the *one* things the *one* thing in our own lives. Your oil, or lack of oil, is contagious to the next generation. Have you been taking enough time in the presence of God to refuel your lamp, your garments with the dew of heaven?

> ***One of the major keys in leading this next generation to worship in the way the Father is seeking is to make sure we are constantly and consistently doing it ourselves.***

This will take effort and an investment of time. It will also take sacrifice and pruning. John 15:1-4 says, *"I am the true vine, and My Father is the vinedresser. Every branch in Me that does not bear fruit He takes away; and every branch that bears fruit He prunes, that it may bear more fruit."* It is time to evaluate our oil and do what is necessary to keep it dripping down to the next generation. If we do not, we are at risk of giving flesh and not oil at all.

This is what I believe has happened in many different ministries of the body. We are giving of ourselves instead of the overflow of the oil of the Father's presence in our own life. This is the warning to the church in Revelation 2:2-4, *"I know your works, your labor, your patience, and that you cannot bear those who are evil. And you have tested those who say they are apostles and are not, and have found them liars; and you have persevered and have patience, and have labored for My name's sake and have not become weary. Nevertheless I have this against you, that you have left your first love."* It is possible to do a lot of good, to labor for the Lord well, but to have lost our own place of worship and intimacy with the Father. In fact, I not only think it is possible, but probable in so many churches and ministries. It's time to prune that we may demand time with the Father. This is true for your personal time, as well as your time within the ministry.

Is it better to raise a generation that has encountered an Easter program every year, but not encountered the resurrected one? To have sung about what Jesus has done, but not encountered what He is doing in their lives? To lead them into a religious activity, or a lifestyle of worship? What oil are you giving the next generation? The Father is beckoning us to lay some things aside and teach them how to encounter His presence. The dark days are getting darker. This generation doesn't need our programs or our flesh; they need the oil of His presence. They need to know how to thrive and walk in a world that is full of the anti-Christ spirit. They need to know how to cry out Abba Father and hear Him respond.

> ***Let's say to a generation, "Imitate me, just as I also imitate Christ" (1 Corinthians 11:1). I implore you to worship as the Father is seeking. Get saturated in the oil and go and lead the next generation to do the same, and see what the Father will do. The oil of His presence running down your garments to the next generation will always bring unity, and unity places a demand on the glory.***

Chapter 7

Moving in the Glory

When Solomon had finished praying, fire came down from heaven and consumed the burnt offering and the sacrifices; and the glory of the LORD filled the temple. And the priests could not enter the house of the LORD, because the glory of the LORD had filled the LORD'S house. When all the children of Israel saw how the fire came down, and the glory of the LORD on the temple, they bowed their faces to the ground on the pavement, and worshiped and praised the LORD, saying: "For He is good, For His mercy endures forever"
(2 Chronicles 7:1-3).

If we, as leaders, will seek to impart purpose for a generation's worship, break open the box on how we define worship to a generation, follow the pattern within the word of God, and saturate our own garments in the oil of His presence, we will see this day come for a generation.

A day of worship so holy, so sovereign, and so out of the box that there will be no words to define it or explain it. That is the fruit of worship the Father is seeking.

> ***Worship with a purpose brings encounter with the Father, and encounter brings faith, and faith brings the glory.***

Encounter defines what a generation believes. The experience must come first before they believe. If you don't believe this, try finding a little child who has never eaten a lemon. If you offer them a lemon, they will boldly put it in their mouth for the first time, encountering its sour taste with humorous distorted facial expressions. Through their experience of taste, they now know that lemons are sour. Now, find someone who has already encountered that lemon and watch their mouth water and lips pucker before they even get it to their lips. Why? Because their encounter has already defined for them what that lemon is going to taste like. Encounters have power to direct our heart - good or bad - and lead us into the decisions we make. Encounters have the power to change how we respond to things. Encounters solidify our faith for what we will believe is real.

"Oh, taste and see that the LORD is good; blessed is the man who trusts in Him!" (Psalm 34:8). This is an experiential invitation to the love of the Father. We cannot expect children to believe in what they cannot encounter. This is why so many fall away from a true redemptive salvation. They receive based upon what they have heard, not what they have experienced.

We have expected children for far too long to believe in what they have never experienced. Jesus is alive...really? Jesus speaks to you...really? Jesus heals...really? One of the most distinct differences between Christianity and other religions is that we serve a *living* God. A living God; A living Father – who is meant to be *experienced*. Jesus was not afraid of revealing Himself to those who doubted. Look at Peter. What angered Jesus was the pompous religious leaders who were determined they knew what they believed, absent of an encounter to give witness to it. If a generation never encounters the reality of the Father, they will not have the faith enough to believe when the reality of the world presses down upon them.

The more you lead your children into worship the Father is seeking, the more they encounter His presence. Psalm 34:8, "Oh, taste and see that the LORD *is* good", becomes a hook in their jaw that draws them back into His presence daily. They begin to hunger for the taste of His presence until worship becomes a lifestyle. In this moment, they become a carrier of heaven wherever they go.

> **Your children will no longer worship to pursue His presence, but worship out of His presence. This is where worship in the garden is realized.**

As your children shift to become heaven carriers, the Father will take His liberty. This is when the glory comes. When they are undone in His presence, and it is no longer them, but *He* who is moving. As I previously mentioned in the last chapter, our goal in worship is to always lead the children into an encounter with the Father in the Most Holy Place. This is where we do nothing, and He does it all. Where we are simply surrendered under His love, and His glory comes and changes things. He shifts atmospheres and cultures and changes lives in a moment. This is the place of miracles, signs, and wonders. The Kingdom of Heaven comes down, and the Father, being an all-consuming fire, burns up anything that is not of Him. This is the pursuit of revival in its purest form. The glory of the

Father makes a demand on everything and everyone in the room. Everything begins to line up with heaven.

In this place where heaven comes down, a transformation takes place. Worship is the road to the Father's presence, and when we touch His presence, we can't help to be changed. I often, when talking about worship to children, speak about what worship does to us. Worship has power. This is why Satan desires to shift our worship to Him. It changes us from the inside out. Humanity is likened to a chameleon lizard. Whatever we touch, we begin to look like. If you surround yourself with the world, you will begin to take on the character and nature of the world. Just the same, if you surround yourself with heaven and the presence of the Holy Father, you will begin to take on the character and nature of Christ.

> **A generation who makes worship a lifestyle and becomes a carrier of heaven, will take on the glory of the Father.**

A shift takes place in their heart; the fruit of true revival. You no longer have to teach them about the fruits of the Spirit, they become a manifestation of the fruits. The intimate relationship between them and the Father spills out, and they are changed from the inside out. We have tried to teach a generation to obtain the character of Christ without relationship. We have done it backwards for so long. Corporately today, we see an adult church that is full of compromise. The lines have been so blurred, we can't tell where the world starts and holiness begins. I believe this is not due to the lack of the Word. Yes, we need the Word of God, but I see too many who sit under the Word week after week and live unholy. If holiness came from hearing the Word of God, the children in the Old Testament would have walked in it. Holiness comes from knowing the Word of God; intimately knowing Jesus. Jesus came as the

Word made flesh, and as we encounter that Word in Sonship worship, we are transformed. We have tried to bring holiness through the written Word alone, and it will never happen. Holiness begins with an encounter.

Holiness brings light. We need a generation who can love a dying world right to the cross. We need a generation who will manifest Jesus out of the overflow of being with Him. This is only obtained through a generation who worships the Father in spirit and in truth. Many have asked why we are not seeing the last day harvest in a last day world. The world is getting darker and darker by the day, and the anti-Christ spirit, in some ways, is taking over the culture. Our children are having sin and perversion flaunted in their faces and are faced with things we, and our parents, couldn't imagine happening. Could it be the light just hasn't been light enough to stand out in a dark world?

> ***The Father is seeking a generation who will worship Him, until the glory comes, so that He can save His children through them.***

But not only save the world, but also save themselves from the world. There has never been a greater need for a generation to worship through the perspective of the love of the Father. I want us to think about the end time prophecies for a moment. According to Revelation 13:13 and Thessalonians 2:1-4, the anti-Christ Spirit (including the Antichrist and False Prophet) will bring miracles, signs, and wonders. There are demonic circles present today that are bringing these things right to the forefront in our culture. As these type of signs and wonders become more prevalent in our society, the worship war will challenge a generation to worship the one in whom performs with, seemingly, the most power. Those who have failed to worship out of the response of the love of the Father will lack the relationship and Spirit required to discern the difference. They will fall prey to Satan's deception.

> ***The discerning difference between the anti-Christ Spirit and God in the end, will be love.***

The anti-Christ Spirit cannot carry the characteristics of the love of the Father. If we teach a generation to shift their focus on worship to the One who is love, they will discern right away what is of God and what isn't.

However, I do want to give a word of warning with this thought. Today, Godly love has been confused with worldly love. Worldly love is conditional, self-exalting, and fleshly in nature. It is a love that satisfies the lust of humanity verses the holiness of God the Father. You see this manifested through the homosexuality and transgender agendas today. Many who claim to be believers have taken on an ideology that says we must accept sin for the sake of love. That is not Godly love. God's love destroys sin to free those enslaved in it. Worldly love fuels sin in order to justify the lust of the flesh. Today right is being called wrong, and wrong, right. Without the reality of Jesus manifested in their life, the world is guaranteed to snatch them away. They will grab hold to what seems real and what feels good.

The Spirit of the Lord is the same with our children as He is with adults. He does not give of Himself partially. Children can encounter His presence and taste of His glory. In fact, I believe they can easier than adults. There are so much less pre-conceived notions with children. When we set the bar of expectations high enough to give them something to reach for, they do. They desire to be part of the body, not the body to come. They simply need someone to disciple them how to pursue a relationship – not a religion. They are a reality generation, and if we are going to expect them to worship a God who is Spirit, we must bring the Sprit into their reality.

I long to see a generation who finds themselves undone like the priest in 1 Kings 8:11: *"The priests could not continue ministering because of the cloud; for the glory of the LORD filled the house of the LORD."* In one second all the programs and good intended traditions go out the window, and God the Father takes over.

> ***I long for the day we walk in to our children's ministry classes and we do NOTHING and He does it all.***

How will that ever happen? When a generation tastes of the goodness of the love of the Father and seeks after Him with their whole life. Let's go for it! Let's shift the way we define worship to a generation and see God find the worship He is seeking after in the hearts of our children.

The weight of our ministry to children is heavy, but let it be said about us – ***that we taught a generation how to move the heart of the Father through worship, and that their impact may remain throughout eternity.***

"Yet for us there is one God, the Father, of whom are all things, and we for Him; and one Lord Jesus Christ, through whom are all things, and through whom we live." 1 Corinthians 8:6

"One God and Father of all, who is over all and through all and in all." Ephesians 4:6

"Father of the fatherless and protector of widows is God in his holy habitation." Psalm 68:5

"But now, O LORD, you are our Father; we are the clay, and you are our potter; we are all the work of your hand." Isaiah 64:8

Do you not believe that I am in the Father and the Father is in me? The words that I say to you I do not speak on my own authority, but the Father who dwells in me does his works. Believe me that I am in the Father and the Father is in me, or else believe on account of the works themselves." John 14:10-11

"For you did not receive the spirit of slavery to fall back into fear, but you have received the Spirit of adoption as sons, by whom we cry, "Abba! Father!" Romans 8:15

"But the Helper, the Holy Spirit, whom the Father will send in my name, he will teach you all things and bring to your remembrance all that I have said to you." John 14:26

"See what kind of love the Father has given to us, that we should be called children of God; and so we are. The reason why the world does not know us is that it did not know him." 1 John 3:1

Our own Children in a moment of worship:

Our Daughter, Hope, under the power and presence of the Jesus in a revival service.

Our Daughter, Faithanna, Interceding under the anointing and presence of Jesus.

Our son, Samuel, preaching at a youth service

Our Isabella, by herself in deep worship

Other children in a moment of worship:

Presence-Driven Family Ministry

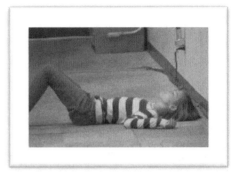

Church resources Recommended

Act of Worship

This resource written as a church worship curriculum, meant to be used right before your children's ministry worship service. However, this is an excellent tool for family worship experiences. All 52 acts of worship in this curriculum are in the Stone Moments Manual for families, but in this resource each one comes with a full teaching. This resource covers the acts of worship from simply raising of your hands, knelling, clapping, and singing, to more of the deeper worship like praying in the spirit and listening for the voice of God.

The Kingdom Of Heaven

13 full lessons curriculum and altar encounters on how to be a citizen of the Kingdom of Heaven. It covers everything from what a kingdom is, the principles of a kingdom, and how to function as a citizen of a kingdom

Living Stones

13 full lessons curriculum and altar encounters to teach a word study of how God has chosen to use stones in the "seen" world, to create a spiritual revelation of who we are and the calling and purpose of each one of us as Living Stones in the "unseen" world.

Radical Worship

13 full lessons curriculum and altar encounters to teach about worship from before the earth was created, to the Garden of Eden, through the Tabernacle of Moses, to the Garden of Gethsemane with Jesus, right to Mary's alabaster box. Deep within the pages of this curriculum you will be lead on a journey to redefine what true biblical worship is all about.

Amazing Grace

13 full lessons curriculum and altar encounters to teach about finding Biblical authentic grace that refutes the popular extreme movements of generations past that formed legalistic law based mindsets, as well as the more recent swing in the other directions that made grace a "get out of jail free" for a compromising and lawless generation. This curriculum brings a holistic and biblical view of grace that encompasses a foundation of grace based upon a biblical perspective of who God is, who we are not, why we need grace through Christ, the right posture to receive grace, and what the work of grace produces in every believer that is yielded to the Holy Spirit.

Malachi Movement Parent's Small Group Course

This is an 8 week course to bring the parents of your church into their God given calling as their children's spiritual leader and teacher. There is a DVD with 8 introduction teachings from me, a facilitator manual, and a parent's workbook.

Family Resources Recommended

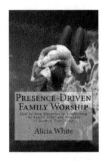

Presence-Driven Family Worship

I highly recommended purchasing this resource for your families within your church to read as you begin to birth presence-driven family ministry. This will help them grab hold of the vision for their families and inspire them to engage in your ministry and in home family worship.

Stone Moments Family Manual

Although written for families, I highly recommended purchasing this resource as you begin hosting family gatherings. It has 72 creative spirit lead acts of worship you can do with your families.

Act of Worship

This resource although written as a church curriculum, is an excellent resource for home. All 52 acts of worship in this curriculum are in the Stone Moments Manual but in this resource each one comes with a full teaching for your families. This resource covers the acts of worship from simply raising of your hands, knelling, clapping, and singing, to more of the deeper worship like praying in the spirit and listening for the voice of God.

Presence-Driven Family Ministry

Malachi Movement Parent's Small Group Course

This is an 8 week course to bring the parents of your church into their God given calling as their children's spiritual leader and teacher. There is a DVD with 8 introduction teachings from me, a facilitator manual, and a parent's workbook.

Radical Worship Family Devotional

Your families will go on a 52 day journey of worship from before the earth was created, to the Garden of Eden, through the Tabernacle of Moses, to the Garden of Gethsemane with Jesus, right to Mary's alabaster box. The Tabernacle teaching in this book came straight out of the pages of this devotional to be shared as a family with discussion questions and presence-driven family worship exercises.

Living Stones Family Devotional

Through a detailed word study of how God has chosen to use stones in the "seen" world, a picture begins to form that reveals who we are as living stones in the "unseen" world according to 1 Peter 2:4. Your families will take a 40 day journey from the Old Testament to the New, discovering mysteries hidden in God's word to find your calling as Living Stones. This devotional is filled with creative spirit lead worship activities that go along with each subject learned.

Amazing Grace Family Devotional

This 52 day devotional is all about helping your families find Biblical authentic grace. This resource brings a holistic view of grace that encompasses a foundation of grace based upon a biblical perspective of who God is, who we are not, why we need grace through Christ, the right posture to receive grace, and what the work of grace produces in every believer and family that is yielded to the Holy Spirit. There are opportunities given for presence-driven family worship in the devotional as well.

Kingdom Family Devotional

This resource is full of 84 days your families can experience learning about our King and the Kingdom of Heaven together. Through the view finder of a kingdom, they will discover their own purpose for being born on this earth and feel a since of belonging to something greater than themselves. Spirit filled acts of worship is all included in this resources for your families as it pertains to the subject.

Worship the Father is Seeking

Made in the USA
Columbia, SC
01 February 2019